"Special Edition for WCDN Conference"

Reverend Dr. Jaerock Lee

GOD THE HEALER

URIM BOOKS

World Christian Doctors Network
WCDN

If you listen carefully
to the voice of the LORD your
God and do what is right in his eyes,
if you pay attention to his commands and
keep all his decrees, I will not bring on you any
of the diseases I brought on the Egyptians,
for I am the LORD, who heals you.
(Exodus 15:26)

GOD THE HEALER by Dr. Jaerock Lee
Published by Urim Books
851, Guro-dong, Guro-gu, Seoul Korea
www.urimbook.com

Previously published in Korean by Urim Books, Seoul, Korea.
Copyright © 1992, ISBN: 978-89-7557-061-2,
ISBN: 978-89-7557-060-5(set)
Translated by Dr. Kooyoung Chung. Used by permission.

First Published March 2005
Second Published January 2007

Edited by Dr. Geumsun Vin
Published in Seoul Korea by Urim Books (Rep.: Seongkeon Vin)
Printed in Seoul, Korea

A Message on Publication

As material civilization and prosperity continue to advance and increase, we find today that people have more time and means to spare. Moreover, in order to achieve healthier and more comfortable lives, people invest time and wealth and pay close attention to a variety of useful information.

However, for man's life, aging, disease, and death are under the sovereignty of God, they cannot be controlled by the might of money or knowledge. In addition, it is an undeniable fact that despite the highly sophisticated medical science produced by man's knowledge accumulated over the centuries, the number of patients suffering from incurable and terminal diseases has been steadily rising.

Throughout the history of the world, there had been countless people of various faiths and knowledge – including Buddha and Confucius – but all of them were silent when faced with this question and none of them was able to avoid aging, disease, and death. This question is bound to sin and the issue of mankind's salvation, neither of which is soluble by man.

Today, there are many hospitals and pharmacies, which are easily accessible and seemingly ready to make our society sickness-free and healthy. Nevertheless, our bodies and world are infested with a variety of diseases ranging from a common flu to diseases of unidentified origins and strains to which there is no cure. People are quick to blame climate and environment or readily perceive it as natural and physiological phenomena, and rely on medication and medical technology.

In order to receive fundamental healing and lead a healthy life, each of us must comprehend from where an illness has originated and how we can receive healing. To the gospel and the truth are always two sides: reserved for people who do not accept them are curse and punishment, while for people who accept them blessing and life wait. It is the will of God for the truth to be hidden from those who, like the Pharisees and teachers of the law, deem themselves wise and intelligent; it is also the will of God for the truth to be revealed to those who are like children, desire it, and open up their hearts (Luke 10:21).

God has plainly promised blessing for those who obey and live by His commands, while He has also recorded in detail of the curse and all types of disease that will be inflicted on those who disobey His commands (Deuteronomy 28:1-68).

By reminding God's Word to unbelievers and even some believers who overlook it, this work seeks to place such individuals on the right path to freedom from sickness and disease.

As much as you hear, read, understand, and make food of God's Word, and by the power from the God of salvation and healing, may you receive healing of sicknesses and diseases large and small, and may health always dwell in you and your family, in the name of our Lord I pray!

Jaerock Lee

The Author

Reverend Dr. Jaerock Lee

He was born in Muan, Jeonnam Province, Republic of Korea, in 1943. In his twenties, Rev. Dr. Lee had suffered from a variety of incurable diseases for seven years and awaited death with no hope for recovery. One day in the spring of 1974, however, he was led to a church by his sister and when he knelt down to pray, the living God immediately healed him of all his diseases.

From the moment Rev. Dr. Lee met the living God through that wonderful experience, he has loved God with all his heart and sincerity, and in 1978 was called to be a servant of God. He prayed fervently so that he could clearly understand the will of God and wholly accomplish it, and obeyed all the Word of God. In 1982, he founded Manmin Joong-ang Church in Seoul, Korea, and countless works of God, including miraculous healings and wonders, have been taking place at his church.

In 1986, Rev. Dr. Lee was ordained as a pastor at the Annual Assembly of Jesus' Sungkyul Church of Korea, and four years later in 1990, his sermons began to be broadcast on the Far East Broadcasting Company, the Asia Broadcast Station, and the Washington Christian Radio System to Australia, Russia, the Philippines, and many more.

Three years later in 1993, Manmin Joong-ang Church was selected as one of the "World's Top 50 Churches" by the *Christian World* magazine (US) and he received an Honorary Doctorate of Divinity from Christian Faith College, Florida, USA, and in 1996 a Ph. D. in Ministry from Kingsway Theological Seminary, Iowa, USA.

Since 1993, Rev. Dr. Lee has taken the lead in world mission through many overseas crusades in Tanzania, Argentina, Uganda, Japan, Pakistan, Kenya, the Philippines, Honduras, India, Russia, Germany, Peru, DR Congo, and New York of the USA and in 2002 he was called a "worldwide pastor" by major Christian newspapers in Korea for his work in various overseas crusades.

As of February 2007, Manmin Joong-ang Church is a congregation of more than 100,000 members and 5,000 domestic and overseas branch churches throughout the globe, and has so far commissioned more than 106 missionaries to 22 countries, including the United States, Russia, Germany, Canada, Japan, China, France, India, Israel, Kenya, and many more.

To this day, Rev. Dr. Lee has written 40 books, including bestsellers *Tasting Eternal Life Before Death, The Message of the Cross, The Measure of Faith, Heaven I & II, Hell,* and *The Power of God,* and his works have been translated into more than 18 languages.

Rev. Dr. Lee is currently leader of many missionary organizations and associations including Chairman, The United Holiness Church of Korea; President, The Nation Evangelization Newspaper; President, Manmin World Mission; Founder, Manmin TV; Founder & Board Chairman, Global Christian Network (GCN); Founder & President, The World Christian Doctors Network (WCDN); and Founder & Chairman, Manmin International Seminary (MIS).

CONTENTS

Chapter 1

The Origin of Disease

and

the Ray of Healing

Malachi 4:2

But for you who revere my name,
the sun of righteousness will rise
with healing in its wings.
And you will go out and leap like
calves released from the stall.

An Underlying Cause of Disease

For people desire to lead happy and healthy lives during their time on this earth, they consume all kinds of food that are known to be helpful for health, and they pay attention to and seek secret methods. Despite the advancement of material civilization and medical science, however, the reality is that the suffering from incurable and terminal diseases cannot be prevented.

Can man not be free from the agony of disease during his time on this earth?

Most people are quick to blame climate and environment or readily perceive disease as a natural or physiological phenomenon, and rely on medication and medical technology. Once the sources of all kinds of diseases and illnesses are determined, however, anyone can be free from them.

The Bible presents to us the fundamental ways by which one can live a life free from disease and, even if one is ill, ways by which he can receive healing:

> *[God] said, "If you listen carefully to the voice of the LORD your God and do what is right in his eyes, if you pay attention to his commands and keep all his decrees, I will not bring on you any of the diseases I brought on the Egyptians, for I am*

the LORD, who heals you" (Exodus 15:26).

This is the faithful Word of God, who controls man's life, death, curse, and blessing, given to us in person.

What, then, is disease and why does one become infected by it? In medical terms, "disease" refers to all kinds of disabilities in various parts of one's body – an unusual or abnormal state of health – and is developed and spread mostly by bacteria. In other words, disease is an abnormal body condition triggered by disease-causing poison or bacteria.

In Exodus 9:8-9 is a description of a process in which the plague of boils was to be brought on Egypt:

> *Then the LORD said to Moses and Aaron, "Take handfuls of soot from a furnace and have Moses toss it into the air in the presence of Pharaoh. It will become fine dust over the whole land of Egypt, and festering boils will break out on men and animals throughout the land."*

In Exodus 11:4-7, we read of God's distinguishing the people of Israel from the people of Egypt. For the Israelites who worshipped God, there was to be no plague, while for the Egyptians who neither worshipped God nor lived by His will, there was to be a plague on their firstborn.

Through the Bible, we learn that even disease is under

the sovereignty of God, that He protects those who revere Him from disease, and that disease will infiltrate those who sin because He will turn His face away from such individuals.

Why, then, are there disease and the suffering from disease? Does this mean that God the Creator made disease at the time of the creation so that man might live in the danger of disease? God the Creator created man and controls everything in the universe in goodness, righteousness, and love.

In Genesis 1:26-28 is the following:

> *Then God said, "Let us make man in our image, in our likeness, and let them rule over the fish of the sea and the birds of the air, over the livestock, over all the earth, and over all the creatures that move along the ground." So God created man in his own image, in the image of God he created him; male and female he created them. God blessed them and said to them, "Be fruitful and increase in number; fill the earth and subdue it. Rule over the fish of the sea and the birds of the air and over every living creature that moves on the ground."*

After creating the most suitable environment for man to live (Genesis 1:3-25), God created man in His own image, blessed them, and allowed them the utmost freedom and authority.

As time passed, people freely enjoyed God-given blessings as they obeyed His commands, and lived in the Garden of Eden in which there were no tears, sorrow, suffering, and disease. As God saw that everything He had made was very good (Genesis 1:31), He gave one command: *"You are free to eat from any tree in the garden; but you must not eat from the tree of the knowledge of good and evil, for when you eat of it you will surely die"* (Genesis 2:16-17).

Yet, when the crafty serpent saw that people had not kept the command of God in their mind but instead neglected it, the serpent tempted Eve, the wife of the first man created. When Adam and Eve ate the fruit from the tree of the knowledge of good and evil and sinned (Genesis 3:1-6), as God had warned, death entered man (Romans 6:23).

After committing the sin of disobedience and as man received the wages of sin and faced death, the spirit in man – his master – also died and the communion between man and God ceased to exist. They were driven from the Garden of Eden and came to live in tears, sorrow, suffering, disease, and death. As everything on the ground was cursed, it produced thorns and thistles and only by the sweat of their brow could they eat their food (Genesis 3:16-24).

Thus, the underlying cause of disease is the original sin brought forth by Adam's disobedience. Had Adam not disobeyed God, he would not have been driven out from the Garden of Eden but have led a healthy life at all times. In other words, through one man every man has become a sinner and come to live in dangers and sufferings of all kinds of diseases. Without first resolving the problem of sin, no one will be declared righteous in God's sight by observing the law (Romans 3:20).

The Sun of Righteousness with Healing in Its Wings

Malachi 4:2 tells us that, *"But for you who revere my name, the sun of righteousness will rise with healing in its wings. And you will go out and leap like calves released from the stall."* Here, "the sun of righteousness" refers to the Messiah.

On the mankind on the path to destruction and suffering from disease, God took pity and redeemed us from all sins through Jesus Christ He had prepared, by allowing Him to be crucified on a cross and all His blood to be shed. Therefore, anyone who has accepted Jesus Christ, received forgiveness for his sins, and reached salvation, can now be free from disease and live a healthy life. By the curse on all things, man had to live in the danger of disease as long as he had breath but by the love and grace of God, a path to the freedom from disease has now opened.

When God's children resist sin to the point of shedding their blood (Hebrews 12:4) and live by His Word, He will protect them with His eyes that are like blazing fire and shield them with the fiery wall of the Holy Spirit so that no poison in the air could ever penetrate their bodies. Even if one falls ill, when he repents and turns from his ways, God will scorch the disease and heal the affected parts. This is the healing by "the sun of righteousness."

Modern medicine has developed ultraviolet therapy, which is widely used today to prevent and cure a variety of diseases. The ultraviolet rays are highly effective for disinfection and cause chemical changes in the body. This therapy can destroy about 99% of E. coli, diphtheria, and Shigella and is also effective for tuberculosis, rickets, anemia, rheumatism, and skin disease. A treatment that is as helpful and powerful as the ultraviolet therapy, however, cannot be applied to all diseases.

Only "the sun of righteousness with healing in its wings" recorded in Scriptures is the ray of power that can heal all diseases. The rays from the sun of righteousness can be used to heal all types of diseases and because it can be applied to all people, the way by which God heals is truly simple yet complete, and essentially the best.

Not long after the founding of my church, a patient on the verge of death and suffering from excruciating pain from paralysis and cancer was brought to me on a stretcher. He was unable to speak because his tongue had stiffened and unable to move his body because the entire body had become paralyzed. Since the doctors had given up, the patient's wife, who had believed in the power of God, urged her husband to surrender everything to Him. Upon realizing that the only way to sustain his life was clinging and pleading to God, the patient tried to worship even as he lay down and his wife also earnestly pleaded in faith and love. As I saw the faith of the two, I also prayed fervently for the man. Soon afterwards, the man who had previously persecuted his wife for believing in Jesus came to repent by rending his heart, and God sent forth the ray of healing, scorched the man's body by the fire of the Holy Spirit, and cleansed his body. Hallelujah! As the underlying cause of the disease was scorched, the man soon began to walk and run, and he became well again. It is needless to say how Manmin members gave glory to God and rejoiced upon experiencing this astonishing work of God's healing.

For You Who Revere My Name

Our God is an almighty God who created everything in the universe by His Word and created man from the dust. Since this kind of God has become our Father, even if we fall ill, when we wholly depend on Him with our faith, He will see and recognize our faith and gladly heal us. There is nothing wrong with being cured at a hospital, but God delights in His children who believe in His omniscience and omnipotence, earnestly call out to Him, receive healing, and give glory to Him.

In 2 Kings 20:1-11 is the story of Hezekiah, king of Judah, who became ill when Assyria invaded his kingdom, but received complete healing three days after he prayed to God and had his life extended by fifteen years.

Through Prophet Isaiah, God tells Hezekiah to *"Put your house in order, because you are going to die; you will not recover"* (2 Kings 20:1; Isaiah 38:1). In other words, Hezekiah was given a death sentence in which he was told to prepare for his death and arrange affairs for his kingdom and family. Yet, Hezekiah immediately turned his face to the wall and prayed to the LORD (2 Kings 20:2). The king had realized that the disease was the result of his relationship with God, put aside everything, and resolved to pray.

As Hezekiah prayed to God fervently and in tears, He tells and promises the king, *"I have heard your prayer and seen your tears; I will add fifteen years to your life. And I will deliver you and this city from the hand of the king of Assyria. I will defend this city"* (Isaiah 38:5-6). We can also assume how earnestly and fervently Hezekiah must have prayed when God told him, "I have heard your prayer and seen your tears."

God who answered Hezekiah's request completely healed the king so that he could go up to the temple of

God in three days. Furthermore, God extended Hezekiah's life by fifteen years and, during the remainder of Hezekiah's life, He kept safe the city of Jerusalem from the threat of Assyria.

For Hezekiah was well aware that the matter of one's living and dying was under God's sovereignty, praying to God was of utmost importance to him. God was delighted in Hezekiah's humble heart and faith, promised the king's healing, and when Hezekiah sought a sign of his healing, He even made the shadow go back the ten steps it had gone down on the stairway of Ahaz (2 Kings 20:11). Our God is a God of healing and a very thoughtful Father who gives to those who seek.

On the contrary, we find in 2 Chronicles 16:12-13 that *"In the thirty-ninth year of his reign Asa was afflicted with a disease in his feet. Though his disease was severe, even in his illness he did not seek help from the LORD, but only from the physicians."* When he initially came to the throne, *"Asa did what was right in the eyes of the LORD, as his father David had done"* (1 Kings 15:11). He was at first a wise ruler but as he gradually lost his faith in God and began to rely more on man, the king could not receive God's help.

When Baasha, king of Israel, invaded Judah, Asa relied on Ben-Hadad, king of Aram, not on God. For this Asa was reproached by Hanani the seer, but he did not turn from his ways and instead imprisoned the seer and oppressed his own people (2 Chronicles 16:7-10).

Before Asa began relying on the king of Aram, God interfered with the army of Aram so that it could not invade Judah. From the time Asa relied on the king of Aram instead of his God, the king of Judah could no longer receive any help from Him. Furthermore, He could not be happy with Asa who sought the help of physicians rather than that of God. That is why Asa died only two years after he was inflicted with the foot disease. Even though Asa professed his faith in God, because he demonstrated no deed of it and failed to call out to God, the almighty God could not do anything for the king.

The ray of healing from our God can heal any types of diseases so that the paralytic can stand and walk, the blind begin to see, the deaf hear, and the dead come back to life. Therefore, because God the Healer has unlimited power, the severity of a disease is unimportant. From a disease that is as minor as a cold to one that is as critical as cancer or AIDS, for God the Healer it is all the same. The more important matter is the kind of heart with which we come before God: whether it is like that of Asa or Hezekiah.

May you accept Jesus Christ, receive the answer to the problem of sin, be deemed righteous by faith, please God with a humble heart and faith accompanied by deed like those of Hezekiah, receive healing to any and all diseases, and always lead a healthy life, in the name of our Lord I pray!

Chapter 2

Do You Want to Get Well?

John 5:5-6

One who was there had been an invalid
for thirty-eight years.
When Jesus saw him lying there
and learned that he had been in this condition
for a long time, he asked him,
"Do you want to get well?"

Do You Want to Get Well?

There are many different cases of people, who had not previously known God, seeking and coming before Him. Some come to Him as they follow their own good conscience while others come to meet Him after having been evangelized. Some others come to find God after experiencing skepticism on life through failures of business or family discord. Still others come before Him with an urgent heart after suffering from excruciating physical pain or the fear of death.

As the invalid who had been suffering from pain for thirty-eight years by a pool called Bethesda had done, in order to wholly commit your illness to God and receive healing, one must desire healing above all else.

In Jerusalem near the Sheep Gate, there was a pool that was in Hebrew called "Bethesda." It was surrounded by five covered colonnades in which the blind, the lame, and the paralyzed gathered and lay there because legend had it that from time to time, an angel of God would come down and stir up the water. It was also believed that the first one to enter the pool after each stir of the water in the pool, whose name meant "The House of Mercy," would be cured of any disease he had.

Upon seeing an invalid of thirty-eight years lying by the pool, and already knowing how long the man had been suffering, Jesus asked him, "Do you want to get well?" The man responded, "Sir…I have no one to help me into the pool when the water is stirred. While I am trying to get in, someone else goes down ahead of me" (John 5:7). Through this, the man confessed to the Lord that even though he earnestly desired healing, he could not come forth on his own. Our Lord saw the heart of the man, said to him, "Get up! Pick up your mat and walk," and at once the man was cured: he picked up his mat and walked (John 5:8).

You Must Accept Jesus Christ

When the man who had been an invalid for thirty-eight years met Jesus Christ, he received healing instantly. As he came to believe in Jesus Christ, the source of true life, the man was forgiven of all his sins and healed of his disease.

Are any of you in anguish from your disease? If you are suffering from diseases and wish to come before God and receive healing, you must first accept Jesus Christ, become God's child, and receive forgiveness in order to remove any barrier between yourself and God. You must then believe that for God is omniscient and omnipotent, He can perform any miracles. You must also believe that we have been redeemed from all our diseases by Jesus' scourging, and that when you seek in the name of Jesus

Christ you will receive healing.

When we ask with this kind of faith, God will hear our prayer of faith and manifest the work of healing. No matter how old or how critical your disease may be, be sure to commit all your problems of disease to God, remembering that you can become whole again in an instant when the God of power heals you.

When the paralytic featured in Mark 2:3-12 first heard that Jesus had come to Capernaum, the man wanted to go before Him. Upon hearing the news of Jesus' healing people with various diseases, driving out evil spirits, and healing lepers, the paralytic thought that if he believed he could also receive healing. When the paralytic realized he was unable to go nearer to Jesus because of a large crowd that had gathered, with the help of his friends he dug through the roof of the house in which Jesus was staying and the mat on which he was lying was lowered before Jesus.

Can you imagine how much the paralytic must have desired to go before Jesus to the extent of having done this? How did Jesus react when the paralytic, who was unable to go from place to place and unable to move around because of the crowd, showed his faith and dedication with the help of his friends? Jesus did not scold the paralytic for his ill-mannered behavior but instead said to him, "Son, your sins are forgiven," and allowed him to stand up and walk right away.

In Proverbs 8:17 God tells us, *"I love those who love*

me, and those who seek me find me." If you want to be free from the anguish of disease, you must first earnestly desire healing, believe in the power of God that can solve the problem of disease, and accept Jesus Christ.

You Must Destroy the Wall of Sin

No matter how much you believe you can be healed by the power of God, He cannot work in you if there is a wall of sin between you and God. That is why in Isaiah 1:15-20, God tells us *"[Even] if you offer many prayers, I will not listen. Your hands are full of blood; wash and make yourselves clean,"* then *"Though your sins are like scarlet, they shall be as white as snow; though they are red as crimson, they shall be like wool."* We also find the following in Isaiah 59:1-3:

> *Surely the arm of the LORD is not too short to save, nor his ear too dull to hear. But your iniquities have separated you from your God; your sins have hidden his face from you, so that he will not hear. For your hands are stained with blood, your fingers with guilt. Your lips have spoken lies, and your tongue mutters wicked things.*

People who do not know God and have not accepted

Jesus Christ, and have been leading lives on their own accord do not realize that they are sinners. When people accept Jesus Christ as their Savior and receive the Holy Spirit as a gift, the Holy Spirit will convict the world of guilt in regard to sin and righteousness and judgment, and they will acknowledge and confess that they are sinners (John 16:8-11).

However, because there are instances in which people do not know in detail what sin is, hence unable to cast off sin and evil in them and receive answers from God, they must first know what constitutes sin in His sight. For all diseases and illnesses come from sin, only when you look back at yourself and destroy the wall of sin can you experience the swift work of healing.

Let us delve into what Scriptures tell us is sin and how we are to destroy the wall of sin.

1. You must repent of not having believed in God and accepted Jesus Christ.

The Bible tells us that our disbelief in God and not accepting Jesus Christ as our Savior constitute sin (John 16:9). Many unbelievers say that they lead good lives but these people cannot know themselves correctly because they do not know the Word of truth – the light of God – and are unable to distinguish right from wrong.

Even if one is confident of having led a good life, when his life is reflected against the truth, which is the Word of the almighty God who has created everything in the universe and controls life, death, curse, and blessing, much unrighteousness and untruths will be found. That is why the Bible tells us that, *"There is no one righteous, not even one"* (Romans 3:10), and that *"no one will be declared righteous in his sight by observing the law"* (Romans 3:20).

When you accept Jesus Christ and become a child of God after you repented of not having believed in God and accepted Jesus Christ, the almighty God will become your Father, and you will thus receive answers to whatever disease you have.

2. You must repent of not having loved your brothers.

The Bible tells us that *"since God so loved us, we also ought to love one another"* (1 John 4:11). It also reminds us that we are to even love our enemies (Matthew 5:44). If we hated our brothers, we would be disobeying the Word of God, and thus sinning.

For Jesus demonstrated His love for the mankind dwelling in sin and evil by being crucified on a cross, it is only right for us to love our parents, children, and brothers and sisters. It is not right in God's sight for us to hate and be unable to forgive because of insignificant yet ill feelings and misunderstandings towards one another.

In Matthew 18:23-35, Jesus gives us the following

parable:

> *Therefore, the kingdom of heaven is like a king who wanted to settle accounts with his servants. As he began the settlement, a man who owed him ten thousand talents was brought to him. Since he was not able to pay, the master ordered that he and his wife and his children and all that he had be sold to repay the debt. The servant fell on his knees before him. "Be patient with me," he begged, "and I will pay back everything." The servant's master took pity on him, canceled the debt and let him go. But when that servant went out, he found one of his fellow servants who owed him a hundred denarii. He grabbed him and began to choke him. "Pay back what you owe me!" he demanded. His fellow servant fell to his knees and begged him, "Be patient with me, and I will pay you back." But he refused. Instead, he went off and had the man thrown into prison until he could pay the debt. When the other servants saw what had happened, they were greatly distressed and went and told their master everything that had happened. Then the master called the servant in. "You wicked servant," he said, "I canceled all that debt of yours because you begged me to. Shouldn't you have had mercy on your fellow servant just as I had on you?" In*

> *anger his master turned him over to the jailers to be tortured, until he should pay back all he owed. This is how my heavenly Father will treat each of you unless you forgive your brother from your heart.*

Even though we have received our Father God's forgiveness and grace, are we unable or unwilling to embrace faults and flaws of our brothers, but instead inclined to develop rivalry, make an enemy, resent, and provoke each other?

God tells us that *"Anyone who hates his brother is a murderer"* (1 John 3:15), *"This is how my heavenly Father will treat each of you unless you forgive your brother from your heart"* (Matthew 18:35), and urges us not to *"grumble against each other, brothers, or you will be judged"* (James 5:9).

We must realize that if we had not loved but instead hated our brothers, then we, too, have sinned and we will not be filled with the Holy Spirit but become afflicted. Therefore, even if our brothers hate and disappoint us, we ought not to hate and disappoint them in return but instead guard our hearts with the truth, understand, and forgive them. Our hearts must be able to offer prayer of love for such brothers and sisters. When we understand, forgive, and love each other with the help of the Holy Spirit, God will also show us His compassion and mercy, and manifest the work of healing.

3. You must repent if you had prayed with greed.

When Jesus healed a boy possessed by a spirit, His disciples asked Him, "Why couldn't we drive it out?" (Mark 9:28) Jesus responded, "[This] kind does not go out except by prayer and fasting" (Mark 9:29).

In order to receive healing of a certain degree, prayer and imploring must also be offered. Yet, prayers for self-interests will not be answered because God does not delight in them. God has commanded us, *"So whether you eat or drink or whatever you do, do it all for the glory of God"* (1 Corinthians 10:31). Therefore, the purpose of our studies and achieving fame or power must all be for the glory of God. We find in James 4:2-3, *"You do not have, because you do not ask God. When you ask, you do not receive, because you ask with wrong motives, that you may spend what you get on your pleasures."*

Asking for healing in order to maintain a healthy life is for the glory of God; you will receive an answer when you ask for it. Yet, if you do not receive healing even when you ask for it, that is because you may be seeking something that is not proper in the truth even though God wants to give you even greater things many times over.

By what kind of prayer will God be delighted? As Jesus in Matthew 6:33 tells us, *"But seek first his kingdom and his righteousness, and all these things will be given to you as well,"* instead of worrying about food, clothes, and the like, we must first please God by offering prayers for

His kingdom and righteousness, and for evangelization and sanctification. Only then will God answer the desires of your heart and give complete healing of your disease.

4. You must repent if you had prayed in doubt.

God is pleased with prayer that shows one's faith. On this we find in Hebrews 11:6, *"And without faith it is impossible to please God, because anyone who comes to him must believe that he exists and that he rewards those who earnestly seek him."* By the same token, James 1:6-7 remind us, *"But when he asks, he must believe and not doubt, because he who doubts is like a wave of the sea, blown and tossed by the wind. That man should not think he will receive anything from the Lord."*

Prayers offered in doubt indicate one's disbelief in the almighty God, disgracing of His power, and turning Him into an incompetent God. You must repent at once, take after forefathers of faith, and pray diligently and fervently to possess faith by which you can believe in your heart.

Many times in the Bible, we find that Jesus loved those who possessed great faith, chose them as His workers, and carried out His ministry through and with them. When people were unable to show their faith, Jesus reproached even His disciples for their little faith (Matthew 8:23-27), but complimented and loved those with great faith, even if they were Gentiles (Matthew 8:10).

How do you pray and what kind of faith do you

possess?

A centurion in Matthew 8:5-13 came up to Jesus and asked Him to heal one of his servants who lay at home paralyzed and in terrible suffering. When Jesus told the centurion, "I will go and heal him," the centurion responded, "Lord, I do not deserve to have you come under my roof. But just say the word, and my servant will be healed," and showed Jesus his great faith. Upon hearing the centurion's remark, Jesus was delighted and complimented him. "I have not found anyone in Israel with such great faith." The centurion's servant was healed at that very hour.

In Mark 5:21-43 is recorded an instance of an astonishing work of healing. When Jesus was by the sea, one of the synagogue rulers named Jairus came up to Him and fell at His feet. "My little daughter is dying," Jairus pleaded with Jesus. "Please come and put your hands on her so that she will be healed and live."

As Jesus was going with Jairus, a woman who had been subject to bleeding for twelve years came up to Him. She had suffered a great deal under the care of many doctors and had spent all she had, yet instead of getting better she grew worse.

The woman had heard that Jesus was nearby and in the midst of the crowd that was following Jesus, she came up behind Him and touched His cloak. For that woman believed, "If I just touch his clothes, I will be healed," when the woman placed her hand on Jesus' cloak, immediately her bleeding stopped and she felt in her body that she was freed from her suffering. When Jesus realized that power had gone out from Him, He asked, "Who touched my clothes?" When the woman confessed the truth, Jesus told the woman, "Daughter, your faith has healed you. Go in peace and be free from your suffering." He gave the woman salvation as well as the blessing of health.

At that time, people from the house of Jairus came and reported, "Your daughter is dead." Jesus assured Jairus and told him, "Don't be afraid; just believe," and continued on to Jairus' house. There, Jesus told the people, "The child is not dead but asleep," and said to the girl, "'Talitha koum!' (which means "Little girl, I say to you, get up!")." The girl stood up at once and began walking.

Believe that when you ask in faith, even a serious disease can be healed and the dead can be revived. If you had prayed in doubt up to this point, receive healing and be strong by repenting of that sin.

5. You must repent of having disobeyed God's commands.

In John 14:21, Jesus tells us, *"Whoever has my commands and obeys them, he is the one who loves me. He who loves me will be loved by my Father, and I too will love him and show myself to him."* In 1 John 3:21-22 we are also reminded, *"Dear friends, if our hearts do not condemn us, we have confidence before God and receive from him anything we ask, because we obey his commands and do what pleases him."* A sinner could not be confident before God. Yet, if our hearts are honorable and faultless when measured against the Word of truth, we can boldly ask God for anything.

Therefore, as a believer of God, you must learn and comprehend the Ten Commandments, which serve as a précis of the sixty-six books of the Bible, and discover how much of your life has been in disobedience of them.

I. Have I ever had in my heart any other gods before God?
II. Have I ever made idols of my possessions, children, health, business, and the like and worshipped them?
III. Have I ever taken the name of God in vain?
IV. Have I always kept the Sabbath holy?
V. Have I always honored my parents?
VI. Have I ever committed physical murders or spiritual murders by hating my brothers and sisters or causing them to sin?
VII. Have I ever committed adultery, even in my heart?
VIII. Have I ever stolen?
IX. Have I ever borne false witness against my neighbors?
X. Have I ever coveted my neighbor's possessions?

In addition, you must also look back and see whether

you have kept God's command by loving your neighbors as you loved yourself. When you obey God's commands and ask Him, the God of power will heal any and all diseases.

6. You must repent for not having sown in God.

As God controls everything in the universe, He has established a set of laws for the spiritual realm and, as a righteous judge He leads and manages all things accordingly.

In Daniel 6, King Darius was put in a difficult position in which he could not save his beloved servant Daniel from the den of lions, even though he was king. Since he had put a decree in his own writing, Darius could not disobey the law he himself had established. If the king were the first to bend the rule and disobey the law, who would heed and serve him? That is why, even though his beloved servant Daniel was about to be thrown into a den of lions in a scheme of evil men, there was nothing Darius could do.

By the same token, as God does not bend the rule and disobey the law He Himself has set, everything in the universe is run in a precise order under His sovereignty. That is why, *"God cannot be mocked. A man reaps what he sows"* (Galatians 6:7).

As much as you sow in prayer, you will receive answers and grow spiritually, and your inner being will be strengthened, and your spirit renewed. If you had been ill or had infirmities but now sow your time in your love for God by diligently participating in all worship services, you will receive the blessing of health and unmistakably feel your body change. If you sow wealth in God, He will protect and shield you from trials and also give you the blessing of greater wealth.

By understanding how important it is to sow in God, when you cast off hopes for this world that is to decay and perish but instead begin amassing your rewards in heaven in true faith, the almighty God will lead you to a healthy life at all times.

With the Word of God, we have thus far examined what has become a wall between God and man, and why we have been living in the anguish of disease. If you had not believed in God and suffered from illness, accept Jesus as your Savior and begin a life in Christ. Fear not those who can kill the flesh. Instead, by fearing the One who can condemn the flesh and the spirit to hell, keep guard of your faith in the God of salvation from persecutions of your parents, siblings, spouse, parents-in-law, and the rest. When God acknowledges your faith, He will work and you can receive the grace of healing.

If you are a believer but suffering from disease, look back at yourself to see if there are any remnants of evil, such as hatred, jealousy, envy, unrighteousness, filth, greed, sinister motive, murder, dispute, gossip, slander, pride, and the like By praying to God and receiving forgiveness in His compassion and mercy, receive also the answer to the problem of your illness.

Many people attempt to bargain with God. They say that if God heals their diseases and illnesses first, they will believe in Jesus and follow Him well. Yet, because God knows the center of each individual's heart, only after cleansing people spiritually will He heal each of them of their physical diseases. By understanding that the thoughts of man and the thoughts of God are different, may you first obey the will of God so that your spirit may get along well as you receive the blessings of healing of your disease, in the name of our Lord I pray!

Chapter 3

God the Healer

Exodus 15:26

If you listen carefully to the voice of the LORD
your God and do what is right in his eyes,
if you pay attention to his commands
and keep all his decrees,
I will not bring on you any of the diseases
I brought on the Egyptians,
for I am the LORD, who heals you.

Why Does Man Fall Ill?

Even though God the Healer wants all His children to live healthy lives, many of them are suffering from the pain of disease, unable to resolve the problem of disease. Just as there is a cause for every result, there is a cause for every disease as well. For any disease can be swiftly cured once the cause is determined, all those who wish to receive healing must first determine the cause of their diseases.

With the Word of God from Exodus 15:26, we shall delve into the cause of disease, and the ways by which we can be set free from disease and live healthy lives.

"The LORD" is a name designated for God, and it stands for "I AM WHO I AM" (Exodus 3:14). The name also indicates that all the other beings are subject to the authority of the Most Revered God. From the way God referred to Himself as "the LORD, who heals you" (Exodus 15:26), we learn of the love of God that frees us from the agony of disease and the power of God that heals disease.

In Exodus 15:26, God promised us, *"If you listen carefully to the voice of the LORD your God and do what is right in his eyes, if you pay attention to his commands and keep all his decrees, I will not bring on you any of the diseases."* Thus, if you have fallen ill, it serves as a proof of your not having carefully listened to His voice, not having done what was right in His eyes, and not having paid attention to His commands.

For God's children are citizens of heaven, they must abide by the law of heaven. However, if heaven's citizens do not obey its laws, God cannot protect them because sin is lawlessness (1 John 3:4). Then, the forces of disease will infiltrate, leaving disobedient children of God under the anguish of disease.

Let us examine in detail the ways by which we could fall ill, the cause of disease, and how the power of God the Healer can cure those of us suffering from disease.

An Instance in which One Falls Ill as a Result of His Sin

Throughout the Bible, God tells us time and again that the cause of disease is sin. John 5:14 reads, *"Later Jesus found [the man He had healed earlier] at the temple and said to him, 'See, you are well again. Stop sinning or something worse may happen to you.'"* This verse reminds us that if the man were to sin, he could fall ill with a more severe disease than he had before, and also that by the sin, people fall ill.

In Deuteronomy 7:12-15, God promised us that *"If you*

pay attention to these laws and are careful to follow them...The LORD will keep you free from every disease...but he will inflict them on all who hate you." In those who hate are evil and sin, and disease will be brought upon such individuals.

In Deuteronomy 28, commonly known as "The Chapter of Blessing," God tells us of the kinds of blessings we will receive when we fully obey our God and carefully follow all His commands. He also tells us of the kinds of curse that will come upon us and overtake us if we do not carefully follow all His commands and decrees.

Especially mentioned in detail are the types of disease to which we will be exposed if we disobey God. They are plague; wasting disease; fever; inflammation; scorching heat and drought; blight and mildew; "boils of Egypt...tumors; festering sores; and the itch, from which you cannot be cured"; madness; blindness; confusion of mind with no one to rescue; and afflictions in knees and legs with painful boils that cannot be cured, spreading from the soles of the feet to the top of the head (Deuteronomy 28:21-35).

By correctly understanding that the cause of disease is sin, if you have fallen ill you must first repent of not having lived by the Word of God and receive forgiveness. Once you receive healing by living according to the Word, you must never sin again.

An Instance in which One Falls Ill Even Though He Does Not Think He Has Sinned

Some people say that even though they have not sinned, they have still fallen ill. Yet, the Word of God tells us that if we do what is right in God's eyes, if we pay attention to His commands and keep all His decrees, then God would not inflict us with any diseases. If we have fallen ill, we have to acknowledge that along the way we had not done what was right in His sight and not kept His decrees.

What, then, is sin that causes diseases?

If one used the healthy body that God had given him without self-control or immorally, disobeyed His commands, committed mistakes, or led a disorganized life, he puts himself at a greater risk of falling ill. To this category of disease also belong a gastroenteric disorder from excessive or an irregular pattern of eating, a liver disease from continued smoking and drinking, and many other kinds of diseases from overworking one's body.

This may not have been a sin from man's point of view, but in the eyes of God it is a sin. Excessive eating is a sin because it shows one's greed and inability to exert self-control. If one has fallen ill from an irregular pattern of eating, his sin is not having led a routine-based life or kept his mealtime, but having abused his body without self-control. If one has fallen ill after consuming food that was not quite ready, his sin is impatience – not having done according to the truth.

If one used a knife without care and cut himself, and the wound became festered, that is also the result of his sin. If he truly loved God, He would have protected the person at all times from accidents. Even if he committed a mistake, God would have provided a way out and, because He works for the good of people who love Him, the body would not have been scarred. Wounds and injuries would have been caused because he had acted hastily and not in a virtuous manner, both of which were not righteous in God's sight, thus making his action sinful.

The same rule applies to smoking and drinking. If one is aware that smoking clouds his mind, damages his bronchi, and causes cancer but is still unable to quit, and if one is aware that toxicity in alcohol damages his bowels and deteriorates his body organs, but is still unable to quit, these are sinful acts. It shows his inability to control himself and his greed, his lack of love for his body, and his not having followed the will of God. How could these not be sinful?

Even if we had not been certain whether all diseases were the result of sin, we can now be certain of it after having examined many different cases and measured them against the Word of God. We must always obey and live by His Word so that we will be set free from disease. In other words, when we do what is right in His eyes, pay attention to His commands, and keep all His decrees, He will protect and shield us from disease at all times.

Diseases Caused by Neurosis and Other Mental Disorders

Statistics tells us that the number of people suffering from neurosis and other mental disorders is on the rise. If people are patient as the Word of God instructs us, and if they forgive, love, and understand according to the truth, they could easily be set free from such diseases. Yet, there is still evil remaining in their hearts and the evil forbids them from living by the Word. The mental anguish deteriorates other body parts and the immune system, eventually leading to disease. When we live by the Word, our emotions will not be stirred, we will not become hot-tempered, and our minds will not be incited.

There are those around us who do not appear evil but good, yet suffer from this kind of diseases. For they restrain themselves from even ordinary expression of emotions, they suffer from a far more severe disease than those who vent their anger and rage. Goodness in the truth is not the agony from the conflict between contrasting emotions; it is instead understanding of each other in forgiveness and love and taking comfort in self-control and endurance.

In addition, when people knowingly commit sins, they come to suffer from mental disease from mental anguish and destruction. For they do not act goodness but fall deeper into evil, their mental suffering creates a disease. We are to know that neurosis and other mental disorders are self-inflicted, having been caused by our own foolish and evil ways. Even in such a case, the God of love will heal all those who seek Him and wish to receive His healing. Moreover, He will also give them hope for heaven and allow them to dwell in true happiness and comfort.

Diseases from the enemy devil are also because of sin

Some people have been possessed by Satan and suffer from all the diseases the enemy devil throws at them. This is because they have forsaken the will of God and gone away from the truth. The reason for a large number of people who are ill, physically disabled, and demon-possessed in families that have worshipped idols extremely is because God loathes idol-worshipping.

In Exodus 20:5-6 we find, *"I, the LORD your God, am a jealous God, punishing the children for the sin of the fathers to the third and fourth generation of those who hate me, but showing love to a thousand generations of those who love me and keep my commandments."* He gave us a special command, forbidding us from worshipping idols. From the Ten Commandments He has given us, by the first two Commandments – *"You shall have no other gods before me"* and *"You shall not make for yourself an idol in the form of anything in heaven above or on the earth beneath or in the waters below"* – we can easily tell how much God detests idol-worshipping.

If parents disobey the will of God and worship idols, their children will naturally follow their lead. If parents do not obey the Word of God and do evil, their children will naturally follow their lead and do evil. When the sin of disobedience reaches the third and fourth generation, as a wage of sin, their descendants will suffer from diseases the enemy devil inflicts them.

Even if parents had worshipped idols but if their children, from the goodness of their hearts, worship God, He will show His love and mercy and bless them. Even if people are currently suffering from the enemy devil's inflicted diseases after having forsaken the will of God and gone astray from the truth, when they repent and turn their ways from sin, God the Healer will cleanse them. Some He will heal immediately; others He will heal a little later; and still others He will heal according to the growth of their faith. The work of healing will take place according to the will of God: if people have unchanging hearts in His eyes, they will be healed right away; however, if their hearts are cunning, they will be healed at a later time.

We will be free from disease when we live in faith

For Moses was more humble than anyone else on the face of the earth (Numbers 12:3) and was faithful in all God's house, he was deemed a trustworthy servant of God (Numbers 12:7). The Bible also tells us that when Moses died at the age of a hundred and twenty years old, his eyes were not weak nor his strength gone (Deuteronomy 34:7). For Abraham was a whole man who obeyed in faith and revered God, he lived up to the age of 175 (Genesis 25:7). Daniel was healthy even though all he ate was vegetables (Daniel 1:12-16), while John the Baptist was robust even though he only ate locusts and wild honey (Matthew 3:4).

One may wonder how people could remain healthy without consuming meat. Yet, when God first created man, He told him to eat only the fruit. In Genesis 2:16-17 God tells the man, *"You are free to eat from any tree in the garden; but you must not eat from the tree of the knowledge of good and evil."* After Adam's disobedience, God had him eat only the plants of the field (Genesis 3:18), and as sin continued to thrive in this world, after the Judgment of the Flood God instructed Noah to eat "[everything] that lives and moves" (Genesis 9:3-4). As man became gradually evil, God permitted them to eat meat, but not any "detestable" food (Leviticus 11; Deuteronomy 14).

In New Testament times, God told us *"to abstain from food sacrificed to idols, from blood, [and] from the meat of strangled animals"* (Acts 15:29). He allowed us to eat food that is beneficial to our health and advised us to abstain from food that is harmful to us; it would be all the more beneficial for us not to eat or drink any food with which God is not pleased. As much as we follow the will of God and live in faith, our bodies will become stronger, diseases will leave us, and no other illness will invade us. Moreover, we will not fall ill when we live in righteousness with faith because two thousand years ago, Jesus Christ came into this world and bore all our heavy burdens. As we believe that by shedding His blood, Jesus redeemed us from our sins and by His scourging and taking up our infirmities (Matthew 8:17) we are healed, it will be done according to our faith (Isaiah 53:5-6; 1 Peter 2:24).

Before we met God, we had no faith. We lived in pursuit of the desires of our sinful nature and suffered from a variety of diseases as a result of our sin. When we live in faith and do everything in righteousness, we will be blessed with physical health.

As the mind is healthy, the body will be healthy. As we dwell in righteousness and act in accordance with the Word of God, our bodies will be filled with the Holy Spirit. Diseases will leave us and as our bodies receive physical health, no disease will infiltrate us. For our bodies will be at peace, feel light, joyful, and healthy, we will not be in want but only be thankful for God's giving us health.

May you act in righteousness and in faith so that as your spirit gets along well, you will be healed of all your diseases and infirmities, and receive health! May you also receive God's abundant love as you obey and live by His Word – all this in the name of our Lord I pray!

Chapter 4

By His Scourging We Are Healed

Isaiah 53:4-5

Surely our griefs He Himself bore, And our sorrows He carried; Yet we ourselves esteemed Him stricken, Smitten of God, and afflicted. But He was pierced for our transgressions, He was crushed for our iniquities; The chastening for our well-being [fell] upon Him, and by His scourging we are healed.(NASB)

Jesus as the Son of God Healed All Diseases

As people navigate their own courses of life, they encounter a variety of problems. Just as the sea is not always calm, on the sea of life are many problems stemming from home, work, business, disease, wealth, and the like. It would not be an exaggeration to state that among these troubles in life, the most significant is disease.

Regardless of the amount of wealth and knowledge an individual may possess, if he is stricken by a critical disease everything for which he has worked throughout his life will be nothing but a bubble. On the one hand, we find that as material civilization advances and wealth increases, man's desire for health is also rising. On the other hand, no matter how far science and medicine may have developed, new and rare strains of diseases – against which man's knowledge is futile – are being continuously discovered and the number of people suffering is steadily increasing. Perhaps that is why there is even a greater emphasis on health today.

Suffering, disease, and death – all stemming out of sin – epitomize the limit of man. As He had done in Old Testament times, God the Healer presents to us today the way by which people who believe in Him can be healed of all diseases, by their faith in Jesus Christ. Let us examine the Bible and see why we receive answers to the problem of disease and lead healthy lives by our faith in Jesus Christ.

When Jesus asked His disciples, "Who do you say I am?" Simon Peter answered, "You are the Christ, the Son of the living God" (Matthew 16:15-16). This response sounds fairly simple, but it also plainly reveals that only Jesus is the Christ.

During His time, a large crowd followed Jesus because He immediately healed people who were ill. They included the demon-possessed, epileptics, paralytics, and others suffering from a variety of diseases. When lepers, people with a fever, the crippled, the blind, and the rest were healed at the touch of Jesus, they began following and serving Him. How marvelous would have been the sight of this? Upon witnessing such miracles and wonders, people believed and accepted Jesus, received answers to problems in life, and the sick experienced the work of healing. Moreover, just as Jesus healed people in His time, anyone who comes before Jesus can also receive healing today.

A man who was not much different from a cripple attended a Friday All-night Worship Service soon after the founding of my church. After an automobile accident, the man had received therapy for a long time at a hospital. However, because tendons in his knees had been extended, he was unable to bend his knee and because his calf would not move, it was impossible for him to walk.

As he listened to the Word preached, he longed to accept Jesus Christ and be healed. When I prayed earnestly for the man, he stood up immediately and began walking and running. Just as a crippled man near a temple gate called Beautiful jumped to his feet and began to walk at Peter's prayer (Acts 3:1-10), a miraculous work of God was manifested.

This serves as a proof that whoever believes in Jesus Christ and receives forgiveness in His name can be wholly healed of all his diseases – even if they could not have been cured by medical science – as his body is renewed and restored. God who is the same yesterday and today and forever (Hebrews 13:8) works in people who believe in His Word and seek according to the measure of their faith, and He heals various diseases, opens the eyes of the blind, and has the crippled stand up.

Anyone who has accepted Jesus Christ, has been forgiven of all their sins, and has become a child of God must now live a life in freedom.

Let us now examine in detail why each of us can live a healthy life when we come to believe in Jesus Christ.

Jesus was Scourged and Shed His Blood

Prior to His crucifixion, Jesus was scourged by Roman soldiers and shed His blood in the court of Pontius Pilate. Roman soldiers of His time were of robust health, extremely strong, and well-trained. After all, they were the soldiers of an empire that ruled the world of its time. The excruciating pain Jesus endured when these strong soldiers stripped and flogged Him cannot be adequately described with words. At each scourging, the whip was wrapped around Jesus' body and snatched away His flesh and blood dripped from His body.

Why did Jesus, the Son of God who is without sin, blame, or flaw, have to be flogged so harshly and bleed for us sinners? Embedded in this event is a spiritual implication of great depths and amazing providence of God.

1 Peter 2:24 tells us that by Jesus' wounds we have been healed. In Isaiah 53:5 we read that by His scourging we are healed (NASB). About two thousand years ago, Jesus the Son of God was scourged to redeem us from the agony of disease and the blood He shed was for our sin of not having lived by the Word of God. When we believe in the Jesus who was scourged and bled, we will have already been freed from our diseases and healed. This is a token of God's astounding love and wisdom.

Therefore, if you are suffering from disease as a child of God, repent of your sins and believe that you have already been healed. For "faith is being sure of what we hope for and certain of what we do not see" (Hebrews 11:1), even if you feel pain in affected parts of your body, by the faith by which you can say, "I have already been healed," it will indeed be healed soon.

During my grade school years, I had hurt one of my ribs and when it recurred from time to time, the pain was so unbearable that I had difficulty in breathing. A year or two after I accepted Jesus Christ, the pain relapsed when I tried to lift a heavy object and I could not even take another step. Nevertheless, because I had experienced and believed in the power of the almighty God, I prayed earnestly, "When I move about soon after I pray, I believe that the pain will have disappeared and I will walk." As I believed only in my almighty God and erased the thought of the pain, I could stand and walk. It was as if the pain had only been in my imagination.

As Jesus told us in Mark 11:24, *"whatever you ask for in prayer, believe that you have received it and it will be yours,"* if we believe that we have already been healed, we will indeed receive healing according to our faith. However, if we think that we have not yet been healed because of the lingering pain, the disease will not be healed. In other words, only when we break the frame of our own thoughts, will everything be done according to our faith.

That is why God tells us that the sinful mind is hostile to God (Romans 8:7), and urges us to take captive every thought to make it obedient to God (2 Corinthians 10:5). Furthermore, in Matthew 8:17 we find that Jesus took up our infirmities and carried our diseases. If you think 'I am weak,' you can only remain weak. Yet, no matter how difficult and exhausted your life may be, if your lips confess, "For I have in me the power and grace of God and for the Holy Spirit governs me, I am not exhausted," exhaustion will fade away and you will transform into a robust person.

If we surely believe in Jesus Christ who took up our infirmities and carried our diseases, we must remember that there is no reason for us to suffer from disease.

When Jesus saw their faith

Now that we have been healed of our diseases by Jesus' scourging, what we need is faith by which we can believe this. Today, many people who had not believed in Jesus Christ come before Him with their diseases. Some people are healed a little after they accept Jesus Christ while others do not show any progress even after months of praying. The latter group of people needs to look back and examine their faith.

With an account featured in Mark 2:1-12, let us explore how the paralytic and his four friends showed their faith, compelled the healing hand of the Lord to set him free from his disease, and gave glory to God.

When Jesus visited Capernaum, the news of His arrival spread quickly and a large crowd gathered. Jesus preached to them the Word of God – the truth – and the crowd paid attention, not wishing to miss a word of Jesus. Just then, four men brought with them a paralytic on a mat but because of the large crowd, they were unable to bring the paralytic closer to Jesus.

Nevertheless, they did not give up. Instead, they went up to the roof of the house in which Jesus was staying, made an opening above Him, dug through it, and lowered the mat on which the paralytic was lying. When Jesus saw their faith, He said to the paralytic, "Son, your sins are forgiven…get up, take your mat and go home," and the paralytic received healing for which he had earnestly desired. When he took his mat and walked out in full view of them all, people were astonished and gave glory to God.

The paralytic had been suffering from such a severe disease that he was unable to move on his own. When the paralytic heard news of Jesus, who had opened the eyes of the blind, stood up the crippled, healed a leper, driven out demons, and healed many others suffering from a variety of diseases, he desperately wanted to meet Jesus. For he had a good heart, when the paralytic heard such news, he longed to meet Jesus once he found out where He would be.

Then one day, the paralytic heard that Jesus had come to Capernaum. Can you imagine how delighted he must have been upon hearing that news? He must have sought after friends who could help him, and his friends, who fortunately had faith of their own, would have readily accepted their friend's request. For the paralytic's friends had also heard the news about Jesus, when their friend earnestly requested them to bring him to Jesus, they consented.

If the paralytic's friends had neglected his request and ridiculed him, saying, "How could you believe in such things when you haven't seen them for yourself?" they would not have gone through all that trouble to help their friend. Yet, because they also had faith, they could bring their friend on the mat, each of them carrying one end of the mat, and even took the trouble to make an opening in the roof of the house.

When they saw the large crowd gathered after having made a difficult journey, and could not squeeze through to get closer to Jesus, how anxious and disheartened must have they been? They must have asked and even pleaded for a small opening. However, because of the large number of people that had gathered, they saw no opening and they were getting desperate. In the end, they decided to go up to the roof of the house in which Jesus was staying, made an opening in it, and lowered their friend lying on a mat in front of Jesus. The paralytic came and met Jesus from the closest distance than anyone else gathered. Through this story, we can learn how earnestly the paralytic and his friends longed to go before Jesus.

We must pay attention to the fact that the paralytic and his friends did not simply go before Jesus. The fact that they went through all that trouble to meet with Him only after hearing news of Him tells us that they believed in the news of Him and the message He taught. Moreover, by overcoming apparent difficulties, enduring, and aggressively approaching Jesus, the paralytic and his friends showed how humble they were when they went before Him.

When people saw the paralytic and his friends going to the roof and making an opening in it, the crowd might have either scorned them or become angry. Perhaps an event we cannot even imagine might have occurred. Yet, to these five people, nothing and no one was to hinder their path. Once they met Jesus, the paralytic would have been healed and they could have easily repaired or compensated the damage in the roof.

Yet, among many people suffering from severe diseases today, it is hard to find the patient himself or his family presenting faith. Instead of approaching Jesus aggressively, they are quick to say, "I am terribly ill. I'd like to go but I am unable," or "So-and-so in my family is so weak that she cannot be moved." It is disheartening to see such passive people who only seem to be waiting for an apple to drop into their mouths from an apple tree. These people, in other words, lack faith.

If people profess their faith in God, there must also be earnestness by which they can show their faith. For one cannot experience the work of God by faith that is received and stored only as knowledge, only when he shows his faith in deed, does his faith become a living faith and will the foundation of faith for receiving God-given spiritual faith be built. Therefore, just as the paralytic received God's work of healing on his foundation of faith, we must also become wise and show Him our foundations of faith – faith itself – so that we, too, may lead lives in which we receive God-given spiritual faith and experience His miracles.

Your sins are forgiven

To the paralytic who came before Him with the aid of his four friends, Jesus said, "Son, your sins are forgiven," and resolved the problem of sin. For one is unable to receive answers when there is a wall of sin between himself and God, Jesus first settled the problem of sin for the paralytic, who had come to him with a foundation of faith.

If we truly profess our faith in God, the Bible tells us with what kinds of attitude we are to come before Him and how we are to act. By obeying such commands as, "Do's," "Do not's," "Keep's," "Cast off's," and the like, an unrighteous person will transform into a righteous person, and a liar will turn into a truthful and honest person. When we obey the Word of the truth, our sins will be cleansed by the blood of our Lord, and when we receive forgiveness, God's protection and answers will come from above.

For all diseases stem from sin, once the problem of sin is settled, the condition in which God's work can be manifested will be established. Just as a light bulb is lit and machinery operates when the electricity enters the anode and exits the cathode, when God sees one's foundation of faith He will declare forgiveness and give him faith from above, thereby producing a miracle.

"I tell you, get up, take your mat and go home." How heartwarming a remark is this? Upon seeing the faith of the paralytic and his four friends, Jesus resolved the problem of sin and the paralytic came to walk right away. He has become, after a long time of desire, whole again. By the same token, if we wish to receive answers not only to disease but to any other problems we have, we must remember to first receive forgiveness and make our hearts clean.

When people had little faith, they might have sought solutions to their illness by relying on medicine and physicians, but now that their faith has grown and they love God and live by His Word, disease does not invade them. Even if they had fallen ill, when they first looked back at themselves, repented from the bottom of their hearts, and turned from their sinful ways, they immediately received healing. I know many have had such experiences.

A while ago, an elder at my church was diagnosed with a ruptured disk and all of a sudden, he was unable to move. At once, he looked back at his life, repented, and received my prayer. The healing work of God took place on the spot and he became well again.

When her daughter was suffering from pyrexia, the mother of the child realized that her hot-temper had been at the root of her child's suffering, and when she repented of it the child became well again.

In order to save all mankind who, because of Adam's disobedience, had been on the path to destruction, God sent Jesus Christ into this world, and allowed Him to be cursed and crucified on a wooden cross on our behalf. That is because the Bible says, *"Without the shedding of blood there is no forgiveness,"* (Hebrews 9:22) and *"Cursed is everyone who is hung on a tree"* (Galatians 3:13).

Now that we know the problem of sin stems from sin, we must repent of all our sins and earnestly believe in Jesus Christ who redeemed us from all our diseases, and by that faith we ought to lead healthy lives. Many brethren today are experiencing healing, testifying to the power of God, and bearing witness to the living God.

This shows us that to whoever accepts Jesus Christ and asks in His name, all the problems of disease can be answered. No matter how severe one's illness may be, when he believes in his heart Jesus Christ who was scourged and shed His blood, an astonishing healing work of God will be manifested.

Faith Perfected by Deed

As the paralytic received healing with the aid of his four friends after they showed Jesus their faith, if we want to receive desires of our hearts, we must also show God our faith that is accompanied by deed, thereby establishing a foundation of faith. In order to help the readers better understand "faith," I will offer a brief explanation.

In one's life in Christ, "faith" can be divided and explained in two categories. "Faith of flesh" or "faith as knowledge" refers to the kind of faith by which one can believe because of things which are visible and only the Word that corresponds with his knowledge and thoughts. On the contrary, "spiritual faith" is the kind of faith by which one can believe even if he cannot see and the Word does not correspond with his knowledge and thoughts.

By "faith of flesh," one believes that something visible has been created only out of something else that is also visible. With "spiritual faith" which one cannot have if he incorporates his own thoughts and knowledge, one believes that something visible can be created out of something else that is not visible. The latter requires the destroying of one's knowledge and thoughts.

Since birth, an incalculable amount of knowledge is registered in each person's brain. Things he sees and hears are registered. Things he learns at home and at school are registered. Things he learns in various surroundings and conditions are registered. Yet, for not every knowledge registered is true, if any of it is contrary to the Word of God, one must naturally cast it off. For instance, at school he learns that every living thing has either broken up or evolved from a monad to a multi-cellular organism, but in the Bible he learns that all living things were created according to their kinds by God. What should he do? The fallacy of the theory of evolution has already been exposed even by science, time and again. How is it possible, even with man's reason, for an ape to have evolved into a human being and a frog to have evolved into a bird of some sort over the span of hundreds of millions of years? Even logic favors the creation.

Likewise, when "faith of flesh" is transformed into "spiritual faith," as your doubts will be thrown away you will come to stand on the rock of faith. In addition, if you profess your faith in God, you must now put the Word you have stored as knowledge into practice. If you profess to believe in God, you must show yourself as the light by keeping the Lord's Day holy, loving your neighbor, and obeying the Word of the truth.

If the paralytic in Mark 2 had stayed at home, he would not have been healed. Yet, for he believed that he would be healed once he came before Jesus, and showed his faith by applying and utilizing every available method, the paralytic could have received healing. Even if an individual wishing to build a house only prays, "Lord, I believe that the house will be built," a hundred or a thousand prayers will not result in the house's being built on its own. He needs to do his share of the work by preparing the foundation, digging up the ground, setting the pillars, and the rest; in short, "deed" is required.

If you or anyone in your family is suffering from disease, believe that God will give forgiveness and manifest the work of healing when He sees everyone in your family united in love, the unity which He will deem the foundation of faith. Some say that because there is a time for everything, there will be a time for healing as well. However, remember that the "time" is when man establishes the foundation of faith before God.

May you receive answers to your illness as well as for everything else you ask, and give glory to God, in the name of our Lord I pray!

Chapter 5

Power to Heal Infirmities

Matthew 10:1

And when he had called unto him his twelve disciples,
he gave them power against unclean spirits,
to cast them out, and to heal all manner of sickness
and all manner of disease. (KJV)

Power to Heal Diseases and Infirmities

There are many ways to prove the living God to unbelievers, and healing of disease is one such method. When people suffering from incurable and terminal diseases, against which the use of medical science is futile, receive healing, they are no longer able to deny the power of God the Creator but come to believe in that power and give glory to Him.

Despite their wealth, authority, fame, and knowledge, many people today are unable to settle the problem of disease and are left in its anguish. Even though a great number of diseases cannot be cured even with the most highly developed form of medical science, when people believe in the almighty God, rely on Him, and commit the problem of disease to Him, all incurable and terminal diseases can be healed. Our God is the omnipotent God, for whom nothing is impossible, and who can create something out of nothing, have a dry stick sprout and bud (Numbers 17:8), and revive the dead (John 11:17-44).

The power of our God can indeed heal any disease and sickness. In Matthew 4:23 we find, *"Jesus went throughout Galilee, teaching in their synagogues, preaching the good news of the kingdom, and healing every disease and sickness among the people,"* and in Matthew 8:17, we read that, *"He [Jesus] took up our infirmities and carried our diseases."* In these passages, "disease," "sickness" and "infirmities" are read.

Here, "infirmities" does not refer to such a relatively light disease as a cold or an illness from fatigue. It is an abnormal condition in which the functions of one's body, body parts, or organs have become paralyzed or degenerated due to an accident or a mistake of his parents or his own. For instance, those who are mute, deaf, blind, crippled, suffering from infantile paralysis (otherwise known as polio), and the rest – those that cannot be cured by knowledge of man – can be classified as "infirmities." In addition to conditions caused by an accident or a mistake of his parents or his own, as in the case of the man born blind in John 9:1-3, there are people who suffer from infirmities so that the glory of God might be manifested. Yet, such cases are rare as most are caused by ignorance and mistakes of man.

When people repent and accept Jesus Christ as they seek to believe in God, He gives them the Holy Spirit as a gift. Along with the Holy Spirit they also receive the right to become God's children. When the Holy Spirit is with them, except in very severe and serious cases, most of diseases are healed. The fact that they have received the Holy Spirit alone allows the fire of the Holy Spirit to descend on them and scorch their wounds. Moreover, even if one suffers from a critical disease, when he earnestly prays in faith, destroys the wall of sin between himself and God, turns from the ways of sin, and repents, he will receive healing according to his faith.

"The fire of the Holy Spirit" refers to the baptism of fire that takes place after one receives the Holy Spirit, and in God's eyes it is His power. When the spiritual eyes of John the Baptist were opened and saw, he described the fire of the Holy Spirit as "the baptism of fire." In Matthew 3:11, John the Baptist said, *"I baptize you with water for repentance. But after me will come one who...will baptize you with the Holy Spirit and with fire."* The baptism of fire does not come at anytime but only when one is filled with the Holy Spirit. Since the fire of the Holy Spirit always descends on him who is filled with the Holy Spirit, all his sins and diseases will be scorched and he will come to live a healthy life.

When the baptism of fire scorches the curse of a disease, most of the diseases are healed; infirmities, however, cannot be scorched even by the baptism of fire. How, then, can infirmities be healed?

All infirmities can be healed only by the God-given power. That is why we find in John 9:32-33, *"Nobody has ever heard of opening the eyes of a man born blind. If [Jesus] were not of God, he could do nothing."*

In Acts 3:1-10 is a scene in which Peter and John, who both had received the power of God, help a man crippled from birth, begging by a temple gate called "Beautiful," stand up. When Peter said to him, *"Silver or gold I do not have, but what I have I give you. In the name of Jesus*

Christ of Nazareth, walk" and took the cripple by his right arm, instantly the man's feet and ankles became strong and he began praising God. When people saw the man who had been previously crippled walking and praising God, they were filled with wonder and amazement.

If one wishes to receive healing, he must possess the faith by which he believes in Jesus Christ. Even though the man crippled may have been only a beggar, because he believed in Jesus Christ he could receive healing when those who had received the power of God prayed for him. That is why Scriptures tells us, *"By faith in the name of Jesus, this man whom you see and know was made strong. It is Jesus' name and the faith that comes through him that has given this complete healing to him, as you can all see"* (Acts 3:16).

In Matthew 10:1, we find that Jesus gave His disciples the power against unclean spirits, to cast them out, and to heal all manner of sickness and all manner of disease. In Old Testament times, God gave power to heal infirmities to His beloved prophets including Moses, Elijah, and Elisha; in New Testament times, God's power was with such apostles as Peter and Paul and faithful workers Stephen and Philip.

Once one receives the power of God nothing is impossible because he can help up a cripple, heal those suffering from infantile paralysis and enable them to walk, have the blind come to see, open the ears of the deaf, and loosen the tongues of deaf-mutes.

Various Ways to Heal Infirmities

1. The Power of God Healed a Deaf and Mute Man

In Mark 7:31-37 is a scene in which the power of God heals a deaf and mute man. When people brought the man to Jesus and begged Him to place His hand on the man, Jesus took the man aside and put His fingers into the man's ears. Then he spit and touched the man's tongue. He looked up to heaven and with a deep sigh said to him, 'Ephphatha!' (which means, 'Be healed!')." Immediately, the man's ears were opened, his tongue was loosened and he began to speak plainly.

Could God, who had created everything in the universe by His Word, not have healed the man by His Word also? Why did Jesus put His fingers into the man's ears? Since a deaf person cannot hear sound and communicates with the sign language, this man would not have been able to possess faith the way others did even if Jesus had spoken in sound. For Jesus knew that the man lacked faith, Jesus put his fingers into the man's ears so that through the touch of the fingers, the man might come to possess faith by which he could be healed. The most important element is the faith by which one believes that he could be healed. Jesus could have healed the man by His Word but because the man was unable to hear, Jesus planted faith and allowed the man to receive healing by implementing such a method.

Why, then, did Jesus spit and touch the man's tongue? The fact that Jesus spit tells us an evil spirit had caused the man to become a mute. If someone spit in your face with no particular reason, how would you accept it? It is an act of defilement and an immoral behavior that utterly disregards one's character. Since spitting in general symbolizes disrespect and debasement for someone, Jesus also spit in order to drive out the evil spirit.

In Genesis, we find that God cursed the serpent to eat dust all the days of its life. This, in other words, refers to God's curse on the enemy devil and Satan, who had instigated the serpent, to make prey of man who had been made from dust. Therefore, since the time of Adam the enemy devil has been striving to make prey of man and seeking every opportunity to torment and devour man. Just as flies, mosquitoes, and maggots inhabit in filthy places, the enemy devil inhabits in people whose hearts are filled with sin, evil, and hot-temper and takes hostage of their minds. We must realize that only those who live and act by the Word of God can be healed of their diseases.

2. The Power of God Healed a Blind Man

In Mark 8:22-25, we find the following:

They came to Bethsaida, and some people

> *brought a blind man and begged Jesus to touch him. He took the blind man by the hand and led him outside the village. When he had spit on the man's eyes and put his hands on him, Jesus asked, "Do you see anything?" He looked up and said, "I see people; they look like trees walking around. Once more Jesus put his hands on the man's eyes. Then his eyes were opened, his sight was restored, and he saw everything clearly.*

When Jesus prayed for this blind man, He spit on the man's eyes. Why, then, did this blind man come to see not the first time Jesus had prayed for him but after Jesus prayed for the second time? By His power, Jesus could have healed the man completely but because the man's faith was little, Jesus prayed for the second time and helped him possess faith. Through this, Jesus teaches us that when some people are unable to receive healing the first time they receive prayer, we ought to pray for such people two, three, even four times until a seed of faith, by which they could come to believe in their healing, can be planted.

Jesus to whom nothing was impossible prayed and prayed again when He knew that the blind man could not be healed by his faith. What should we do? With more imploring and praying, we ought to endure until we receive healing.

In John 9:6-9 is a man born blind who received healing

after Jesus spit on the ground, made some mud with His saliva, and put the mud on his eyes. Why did Jesus heal him by spitting on the ground, making some mud with His saliva, and putting on the man's eyes? The saliva here does not refer to anything unclean; Jesus spit on the ground so that he could make mud and put it on the blind man's eyes. Jesus made mud with His saliva also because water was scarce. In case of a boil or a swelling developing or an insect bite on their children, parents oftentimes put their own saliva in an affectionate way. We ought to comprehend the love of our Lord who used a variety of means to help the weak possess faith.

As Jesus put some mud on the blind man's eyes, the man felt the sensation of the mud in his eyes and came to possess faith by which he could be healed. After Jesus gave faith to the blind man whose own faith had been little, by His power He opened the man's eyes.

Jesus tells us that, *"Unless you people see miraculous signs and wonders, you will never believe"* (John 4:48). Today, it is impossible to help people possess the kind of faith by which one can believe only with the Word in the Bible, without witnessing the miracles of healing and wonders. In an age in which science and man's knowledge have advanced tremendously, it is extremely difficult to possess spiritual faith to believe in an invisible God. "Seeing is believing," we have often heard. Likewise, because people's faith will grow and the work of healing will take place all the more rapidly when they see tangible evidences of the living God, "miraculous signs and wonders" are absolutely necessary.

3. The Power of God Healed a Cripple

As Jesus had preached the Good News and healed people suffering from all manner of sickness and all manner of disease, His disciples also manifested the power of God.

When Peter commanded a crippled beggar, "In the name of Jesus Christ of Nazareth, walk" and took him by the right hand, immediately the man's feet and ankles became strong, and he jumped to his feet and began to walk (Acts 3:6-10). As people saw the miraculous signs and wonders Peter manifested after receiving God's power, more people came to believe in the Lord. They even brought the sick into the streets and laid them on beds and mats so that at least Peter's shadow might fall on some of them as he passed by. Crowds gathered also from the towns around Jerusalem, bringing their sick and those tormented by demons, and all of them were healed (Acts 5:14-16).

In Acts 8:5-8 we find, *"Philip went down to a city in Samaria and proclaimed the Christ there. When the crowds heard Philip and saw the miraculous signs he did, they all paid close attention to what he said. With shrieks, evil spirits came out of many, and many paralytics and cripples were healed. So there was great joy in that city"*

(Acts 8:5-8).

In Acts 14:8-12, we read of a man crippled in his feet, who was lame from birth and had never walked. After he listened to Paul's message and came to possess faith by which he could receive salvation, when Paul commanded, "Stand up on your feet!" right away, the man jumped up and began to walk. Those who witnessed this incident claimed that "The gods have come down to us in human form!"

In Acts 19:11-12 we see that *"God did extraordinary miracles through Paul, so that even handkerchiefs and aprons that had touched him were taken to the sick, and their illnesses were cured and the evil spirits left them."* How astonishing and wonderful is the power of God?

Through people whose hearts have achieved sanctification and complete love as did Peter, Paul, and Philip and Stephen, the power of God is manifested even today. When people come before God with faith wishing to have their infirmites healed, they can be healed by receiving prayer from God's servants through whom He works.

Since the founding of Manmin, the living God has allowed me to manifest a variety of miraculous signs and wonders, planted faith in the hearts of the members, and brought great revival.

There was once a woman who had been the subject of her alcoholic husband's abuse. When her optic nerves had become paralyzed and doctors had given up hope after severe physical abuse, the woman came to Manmin after hearing news of it. As she diligently participated in worship services and earnestly prayed for healing, she received my prayer and could see again. The power of God had completely repaired the optic nerves which at one time seemed permanently lost.

On another occasion, there was a man who had suffered from a severe injury in which eight places on his backbone had been crushed. As the lower part of his body had become paralyzed, he was on the verge of having both of his legs amputated. After accepting Jesus Christ, he could avert the amputation but still had to rely on crutches. He then began attending Manmin Prayer Center meetings and a little later during a Friday All-night Worship Service, after receiving my prayer the man threw away his crutches, came to walk on his two feet, and has since become a messenger of the gospel.

The power of God can completely heal infirmities medical science is unable to cure. In John 16:23, Jesus promises us, *"I tell you the truth, my Father will give you whatever you ask in my name."*

May you believe in the amazing power of God, earnestly seek it, receive the answer to all the problems of your disease, and become a messenger who carries the Good News of the living and almighty God, in the name of our Lord I pray!

Chapter 6

Ways to Heal the Demon-possessed

Mark 9:28-29

After Jesus had gone indoors, his disciples asked him privately, "Why couldn't we drive it out?" He replied, "This kind can come out only by prayer."

In the Last Days Love Grows Cold

The advancement of modern scientific civilization and development of industry have brought forth material prosperity and allowed people to pursue more comfort and benefit. At the same time, these two factors have resulted in alienation, overflowing selfishness, betrayal, and an inferiority complex among people, as love abates while understanding and forgiveness are hard to find.

As the Bible had predicted, *"Because of the increase of wickedness, the love of most will grow cold,"* at a time when wickedness thrives and love grows cold, one of the most serious problems in our society today is the increasing number of people suffering from such mental disorders as nervous breakdown and schizophrenia.

Mental institutions isolate many patients who are unable to lead normal lives but they have not yet found appropriate cure. If no progress is made after years of treatment, families become weary and in many cases ignore or abandon patients like orphans. These patients, living away and without families, are unable to function the way normal people do. Although they require true love from their loved ones, not many people show their love to such individuals.

We find in the Bible many instances in which Jesus healed people possessed by demons. Why have they been recorded in Scriptures? As the end of the age draws near, love grows cold and Satan torments people, causes them to suffer from mental disorders, and adopts them as the devil's children. Satan torments, sickens, confuses, and taints with sin and evil the minds of people. For the society is drenched in sin and evil, people are quick to envy, quarrel, hate, and murder one another. As the last days draw nearer, Christians must be able to distinguish truth from untruth, keep guard of their faith, and lead healthy lives physically and mentally.

Let us examine the cause behind Satan's instigation and torment, as well as the increasing number of people possessed by Satan and demons and suffering from mental disorders in our modern society in which scientific civilization has greatly advanced.

The Process of Becoming Possessed by Satan

Everyone has conscience and most people behave and live according to their conscience, but each individual's standard of conscience and ensuing results that follow differ from person to person. This is because each person has been born and raised in different environments and conditions, has seen, heard, and learned different things from parents, home, and school, and has registered different information.

On the one hand, the Word of God, which is the truth,

tells us, *"Do not be overcome by evil, but overcome evil with good"* (Romans 12:21), and urges us, *"Do not resist an evil person. If someone strikes you on the right cheek, turn to him the other also"* (Matthew 5:39). Since the Word teaches love and forgiveness, a standard of judgment "Losing is winning" develops in those who believe it. On the other hand, if one has learned that he should retaliate when he is struck, he will reach a judgment which dictates that resisting is a brave act while avoiding without resisting is cowardly. Three factors – each individual's standard of judgment, whether one had lived a righteous or unrighteous life, and how much he had compromised with the world – will form different consciences in different people.

For people have led their lives differently and their consciences are thus different, God's enemy Satan uses this to tempt people to live according to the sinful nature, contrary to righteousness and good, by stirring evil thoughts and instigating them to sin.

In people's hearts are a conflict between the desire of the Holy Spirit by which they are to live by the law of God, and the desire of the sinful nature by which people are compelled to pursue fleshly desires. That is why God urges us in Galatians 5:16-17, *"So, I say, live by the Spirit, and you will not gratify the desire of the sinful nature. For the sinful nature desires what is contrary to the Spirit, and the Spirit what is contrary to the sinful nature. They are in conflict with each other, so that you do not do what you want."*

If we live by the desires of the Holy Spirit we will inherit the kingdom of God; if we follow the desires of the sinful nature and do not live by the Word of God, we will not inherit His kingdom. That is why God warned us as follows in Galatians 5:19-21:

> *The acts of the sinful nature are obvious: sexual immorality, impurity and debauchery; idolatry and witchcraft; hatred, discord, jealousy, fits of rage, selfish ambition, dissensions, factions and envy; drunkenness, orgies, and the like. I warn you, as I did before, that those who live like this will not inherit the kingdom of God.*

How, then, do people become possessed by demons? Through one's thoughts, Satan stirs desires of the sinful nature in an individual whose heart is filled with the sinful nature. If he is unable to control his mind and does acts of the sinful nature, a sense of guilt settles in and his heart will grow more evil. When such acts of the sinful nature add up, in the end the person will be unable to control himself and instead do whatever Satan instigates him to do. Such an individual is said to be "possessed" by Satan.

For instance, let us assume there is a lazy man who does not like to work, but instead prefers drinking and wasting his time. On such an individual, Satan will instigate and control his mind so that he will stick to drinking and wasting his time feeling that working is burdensome. Satan will also drive him away from goodness which is the truth, rob him of energy to develop his life, and turn him into an incompetent and useless person. As he lives and behaves according to the thought of Satan, the man is unable to escape from Satan. Moreover, as his heart grows more evil and he has already given himself up to evil thoughts, instead of controlling his heart he will do whatever pleases him. If he wants to get angry, he will get angry to his satisfaction; if he wants to fight or argue, he will fight and argue as much as he likes; and if he wants to drink, he will be unable to prevent himself from drinking. When this accumulates, from a certain point on he will not be able to control his thoughts and heart and find that all things are against his will. After this process, he becomes possessed by demons.

The Cause of the demon-possession

There are two main reasons for one to be instigated by Satan and later possessed by demons.

1. Parents

If parents had left God, worshipped idols which God detests and finds abominable, or done something extraordinarily evil, then the forces of evil spirits will infiltrate their children and if left unchecked, they will be possessed by demons. In such a case, the parents must come before God, thoroughly repent of their sins, turn from their sinful ways, and implore of God on behalf of their children. God will then see the center of the parents' hearts and manifest the work of healing, thereby loosening the chains of injustice.

2. Oneself

Regardless of sins of parents, one can be possessed by demons due to his own untruths, including evil, pride, and the rest. Since the individual cannot pray and repent on his own, when he receives prayer from a servant of God who manifests His power, the chains of injustice can be loosened. When demons are driven out and he comes to his senses, he should be taught the Word of God so that his heart that was once drenched in sin and evil will be wiped away and will become a heart of the truth.

Therefore, if one of the family members or relatives is possessed by demons, the family must designate an individual who will pray on that person's behalf. This is because the heart and mind of the demon-possessed person are being controlled by demons and he is unable to do anything according to his own will. He can neither pray nor listen to the Word of the truth; he thus cannot live by the truth. Therefore, the entire family or even just one person from the family must pray for him in love and compassion so that the demon-possessed member of the family can now live in faith. When God sees the devotion and love in that family, He will reveal the work of healing. Jesus told us to love our neighbor as ourselves (Luke 10:27). If we are unable to pray and devote for a member of our own family who is possessed by demons, how can we be said to love our neighbors?

When the family and friends of the one who is possessed by demons determine the cause, repent, pray in the faith of God's power, devote in love, and plant the seed of faith, then the forces of demons will be driven away and their loved one will transform into a man of the truth, whom God will shield and protect against demons.

Ways to Heal People Possessed by Demons

In many parts of the Bible are accounts of the healing of people possessed by demons. Let us examine how they received healing.

1. You must repulse the forces of demons.

In Mark 5:1-20 we find a man *"who lived in the tombs, [whom] no one could bind...not even with a chain."* We also learn that, *"Night and day among the tombs and in the hills he would cry out and cut himself with stones. When he saw Jesus from a distance, he ran and fell on his knees in front of him. He shouted at the top of his voice, 'What do you want with me, Jesus, Son of the Most High God? Swear to God that you won't torture me!'"* (Mark 5:5-7).

This was in response to what Jesus had commanded, "Come out of this man, you unclean spirit!" This scene tells us that even though people did not know that Jesus was the Son of God, the unclean spirit knew exactly who Jesus was and what kind of power He had.

Jesus then asked, "What is your name?" and the demon-possessed man answered, "My name is Legion, for we are many." He also begged Jesus again and again not to send them out of the area and then begged Him to send them into pigs. Jesus did not ask for the name not because he did not know; He asked for the name as a judge interrogating the unclean spirit. Moreover, "Legion" means that a great number of demons were holding the man hostage.

Jesus allowed the "Legion" to enter a herd of pigs, which rushed down the steep bank into the lake and were drowned. When we drive out demons, we must do it with the Word of the truth, which is symbolized by water. When people saw the man, who could not be contained by the power of man, completely healed, sitting there, dressed and in his right mind, they became afraid.

How should we drive out demons today? They should be driven out in the name of Jesus Christ to the water, which symbolizes the Word, or the fire, which symbolizes the Holy Spirit, so that their power will be lost. Yet, since demons are spiritual beings, they will be driven out when a person with power to drive out demons prays. When an individual with no faith attempts to drive them out, demons in turn will belittle or jeer at him. Therefore, in order to heal someone possessed by demons, a man of God with the power to drive them out must pray for him.

However, occasionally demons will not be driven out even when a man of God drives them out in the name of Jesus Christ. That is because the individual possessed by demons had blasphemed or spoken against the Holy Spirit (Matthew 12:31; Luke 12:10). Healing cannot be manifested to some demon-possessed people when they deliberately keep on sinning after they have received the knowledge of the truth (Hebrews 10:26).

Moreover, in Hebrews 6:4-6 we find, *"It is impossible for those who have once been enlightened, who have tasted the heavenly gift, who have shared in the Holy Spirit, who have tasted the goodness of the word of God and the powers of the coming age, if they fall away, to be brought back to repentance, to their loss they are crucifying the Son of God all over again and subjecting him to public disgrace."*

Now that we have learned of this, we must guard ourselves so that we may never commit sins for which we could not receive forgiveness. We must also distinguish in truth whether or not someone possessed by demons can be healed by prayer.

2. Arm yourself with the truth.

Once demons are driven out from them, people must fill their hearts with life and truth by diligently reading the Word of God, praising, and praying. Even if demons are driven out, if people continue to live in sin without arming themselves with the truth, the driven demons will return and this time, they will be accompanied by demons that are more wicked. Remember that people's condition will be far worse than the first time demons had entered them.

In Matthew 12:43-45, Jesus tells us the following:

> *When an evil spirit comes out of a man, it goes through arid places seeking rest and does not find it. Then it says, "I will return to the house I left." When it arrives, it finds the house unoccupied, swept clean and put in order. Then it goes and takes with it seven other spirits more wicked than itself, and they go in and live there. And the final condition of that man is worse than the first.*

Demons are not to be driven out carelessly. Furthermore, after demons are driven out, friends and family of the one who had been possessed by demons ought to understand that the person now requires care with greater love than before. They must look after him in devotion and sacrifice and arm him with the truth until complete healing is received.

Everything is Possible for Him Who Believes

In Mark 9:17-27 is an account of Jesus' healing of a son possessed by a spirit that robbed him of speech and suffering from epilepsy after seeing the faith of his father. Let us briefly examine how the son received healing.

1. The family must show their faith.

A son in Mark 9 had been a mute and deaf since childhood because of demon-possession. He could not understand a word and communication was impossible with him. Moreover, it was difficult to determine when and where the symptoms of epilepsy would occur. His father, therefore, always lived in fear and agony, with all hopes in life lost.

Then the father heard of a man from Galilee who had been manifesting miracles of reviving the dead, and healing various kinds of diseases. A ray of hope began to pierce the man's despair. If the news were right, the father believed, this man from Galilee could heal his son, too. In search of good luck, the father brought his son before

Jesus and said to Him, "[If] you can do anything, take pity on us and help us."

Upon hearing the father's earnest request, Jesus said, "'If you can?' Everything is possible for him who believes," and rebuked the father for his little faith. The father had heard the news but had not believed it in his heart. If the father had been aware that Jesus as the Son of God was almighty and the truth itself, he would not have said "If." In order to teach us that it is impossible to please God without faith and that it is impossible to receive answers without complete faith by which one can believe, Jesus said "'If you can?'" as he rebuked the father for his "little faith."

Faith in general can be divided into two kinds. By "faith of flesh" or "faith as knowledge," one can believe in what he sees. The kind of faith by which one can believe without seeing is "spiritual faith," "true faith," "living faith," or "faith accompanied by deed." This kind of faith can create something from nothing. The definition of "faith" according to the Bible is "being sure of what we hope for and certain of what we do not see" (Hebrews 11:1).

When people suffer from diseases curable by man, they can be healed as their diseases are scorched by the fire of the Holy Spirit when they show their faith and are filled with the Holy Spirit. If a beginner in the life of faith becomes ill, he can be healed when he opens up his heart, listens to the Word, and shows his faith. If a mature Christian with faith becomes ill, he can be healed when he turns his ways through repentance.

When people suffer from diseases that cannot be cured by medical science, they must show faith that is accordingly greater. If a mature Christian with faith becomes ill, he can be healed when he opens up his heart, repents by rending his heart, and offers earnest prayer. If someone with little or no faith becomes ill, he will not be healed until he is given faith and according to the growth of his faith, the work of healing will be manifested.

Those who are physically disabled, whose bodies are deformed, and hereditary diseases can only be healed by God's miracles. Thus, they must show God dedication and the faith by which they can love and please Him.

Only then will God acknowledge their faith and manifest healing. When people show their ardent faith to God – the way Bartimaeus earnestly called out to Jesus (Mark 10:46-52), the way a centurion showed Jesus his great faith (Matthew 8:5-13), and the way the paralytic and his four friends showed faith and dedication (Mark 2:3-12) – God will give them healing.

Likewise, since people who are possessed by demons cannot be healed without the work of God and are unable to show their faith, in order to bring down healing from heaven, other members of their family must believe in the almighty God and come before Him.

2. People must possess the faith by which they can believe.

The father of the son who had long been possessed by a demon was initially rebuked by Jesus for his little faith. When Jesus said with certainty, "Everything is possible for him who believes" to the man, the father's lips gave a positive confession, "I do believe." However, his belief was limited to knowledge. That is why the father begged Jesus, "[Help] me overcome my unbelief!" (Mark 9:24) Upon hearing the plea of the father, of whose sincere heart, earnest prayer, and faith Jesus knew, He gave the father the faith by which he could now believe.

By the same token, by calling out to God we can receive the faith by which we can believe and with this kind of faith, we will become fit to receive answers to our problems, and "the impossible" will become "the possible."

Once the father came to possess the faith by which he could believe, when Jesus commanded, "You deaf and mute spirit, I command you, come out of him and never enter him again," the evil spirit left the son with a shriek (Mark 9:25-27). As the father's lips begged for the faith by which he could believe and desired God's intervention – even after Jesus had rebuked him – Jesus manifested an astounding work of healing.

Jesus even answered and gave complete healing to a

father's son who had been possessed by a spirit that had robbed him of speech, and had been suffering from epilepsy so that he often fell, foamed at the mouth, gnashed his teeth, and became rigid. Then, to those who believe in the power of God by which everything is possible and live by His Word, would He not allow everything to go well and lead them to live healthy lives?

Soon after the founding of Manmin, a young man from Gang-won Province visited the church after having heard the news about it. The young man thought that he was serving God faithfully as a Sunday School teacher and a member of the choir. However, because he was extremely proud and did not cast off evil in his heart but instead accumulated sin, the young man was suffering after a demon entered his unclean heart and began dwelling in it. The work of healing was manifested at the earnest prayer and dedication of his father. After determining the identity of the demon and driving it out by prayer, the young man foamed at the mouth, flipped on his back, and gave out a terrible odor. After this incident, the young man's life renewed as he armed himself with the truth at Manmin. Today, he is faithfully serving his church back in Gang-won and is giving glory to God by sharing grace of the testimony of his healing with countless people.

May you come to understand that the scope of God's work is limitless and that everything is possible by it, so that when you seek in prayer you will become not only a blessed child of God but also His cherished saint whose all matters go well at all times, in the name of our Lord I pray!

Chapter 7

Naaman the Leper's Faith and Obedience

2 Kings 5:9-14

So Naaman went with his horses and chariots
and stopped at the door of Elisha's house.
Elisha sent a messenger to say to him,
"Go, wash yourself seven times in the Jordan,
and your flesh will be restored
and you will be cleansed." ...
So he went down and dipped himself
in the Jordan seven times,
as the man of God had told him,
and his flesh was restored
and became clean like that of a young boy.

General Naaman the Leper

During our lifetime, we encounter problems big and small. At times we face problems that are beyond man's capabilities.

In a country called Aram north of Israel, there was a commander of the army named Naaman. He had led Aram's army to victory at the country's most critical hour. Naaman loved his country and faithfully served his king. Even though the king highly regarded Naaman, the general was in anguish due to a secret of which no one else knew.

What was the cause of his anguish? Naaman was in agony not because he lacked wealth or fame. Naaman felt afflicted and found no happiness in life because he had leprosy, an incurable disease which the medicine of his time was unable to cure.

During Naaman's time, people suffering from leprosy were deemed unclean. They were forced to live in isolation outside the city limits. Naaman's suffering was more unbearable because, in addition to the pain, there were other problems that accompanied the disease. Symptoms of leprosy included spots on the body, especially on one's face, exterior of his arms and legs, the insteps of his feet, as well as degeneration of the senses. In severe cases, eyebrows, fingernails, and toenails fell off and one's overall appearance would turn ghastly.

Then one day, Naaman who had been inflicted by an incurable disease and unable to find joy in life heard good news. According to a young girl taken captive from Israel who was serving his wife, there was a prophet in Samaria who would cure Naaman's leprosy. For there was nothing he would not do to receive healing, Naaman told his king of the disease he had and what he had heard from his maidservant. Upon hearing that his faithful general would be healed of leprosy if he went before a prophet in Samaria, the king eagerly helped Naaman and even wrote a letter to the king of Israel on Naaman's behalf.

Naaman left for Israel with ten talents of silver, six thousand shekels of gold and ten sets of clothing and the king's letter, which read, "With this letter I am sending my servant Naaman to you so that you may cure him of his leprosy." At the time, Aram was a stronger nation than Israel was. Upon reading the letter from the king of Aram, the king of Israel tore his robes and said, "Am I God? Why does this fellow send someone to me to be cured of his leprosy? See how he is trying to pick a quarrel with me!"

When Israel's prophet Elisha heard this news, he came before the king and said, "Have the man come to me and he will know that there is a prophet in Israel." When the king of Israel sent Naaman to Elisha's house, the prophet did not meet with the general but only said through a messenger, "Go, wash yourself seven times in the Jordan, and your flesh will be restored and you will be cleansed."

How awkward must it have been for Naaman, who had gone with his horses and chariots to Elisha's house, only to find the prophet neither welcoming nor meeting with him? The general became angry. He had thought that if a commander of the army of a country stronger than Israel had paid a visit, the prophet would have cordially welcomed and laid his hands on him. Instead, Naaman received a cold reception from the prophet and was told to wash himself in a river that was as small and filthy as the Jordan River.

In a rage, Naaman thought of returning home, saying, "Are not Abana and Pharpar, the rivers of Damascus, better than any of the waters in Israel? Couldn't I wash in them and be cleansed?" As he prepared for his journey home, Naaman's servants pleaded with him. "My father, if the prophet had told you to do some great thing, would you not have done it? How much more, then, when he tells you, 'Wash and be cleansed'!" They urged their master to obey Elisha's instructions.

What happened when Naaman dipped himself in the Jordan River seven times, as Elisha had instructed him? His flesh became clean like that of a young boy. The leprosy that had given Naaman so much agony was completely healed. When a disease incurable by man had been completely healed by Naaman's obedience to a man of God, the general came to acknowledge the living God and Elisha, a man of God.

After experiencing the power of the living God – God the Healer of leprosy – Naaman went back to Elisha, confessed, "Now I know that there is no God in all the world except in Israel…your servant will never again make burnt offerings and sacrifices to any other god but the LORD," and gave glory to God (2 Kings 5:15-17).

Naaman's Faith and Deed

Let us now examine faith and deed of Naaman, who met God the Healer and was cured of an incurable disease.

1. Naaman's Good Conscience

Some people readily accept and believe in the words of others while others tend to unconditionally doubt and distrust other people on the other hand. For Naaman had a good conscience, he did not disregard other people's words but kindly accepted them. He could go to Israel, obey Elisha's instructions, and receive healing because he had not neglected but paid close attention to and believed in the words of a young girl serving his wife. When this young girl, who had been taken captive from Israel, said to his wife, "If only my master would see the prophet who is in Samaria! He would cure him of his leprosy," Naaman believed her. Suppose you were in Naaman's position.

What would you have done? Would you have wholly accepted her words?

Despite the advancement of modern medicine today, there are many diseases against which medicine is useless. If you told others that you have been healed of incurable diseases by God or that you have been healed after receiving prayer, how many people do you think would believe you? Naaman believed in the words of the young girl, went before his king for permission, went to Israel, and received healing of his leprosy. In other words, because Naaman had a good conscience, he could accept the words of the young girl when she evangelized to him and act accordingly. We must also realize that we can receive answers to our problems only when we believe in the preaching and come before God like Naaman.

2. Naaman Shattered His Thoughts

When Naaman went to Israel with the aid of his king and arrived at the house of Elisha, a prophet who could heal leprosy, he received a cold reception. He became evidently angry when Elisha, who in the eyes of the unbelieving Naaman had no fame or social status, did not welcome a faithful servant of the king of Aram, and told Naaman – through a messenger – to wash himself in the Jordan River seven times. Naaman was enraged because he had been sent personally by the king of Aram. Furthermore, Elisha did not even put his hand on the spot but instead told Naaman that he could be cleansed when he washed himself in a river that was as small and filthy as the Jordan River.

Naaman became angry at Elisha and the prophet's action, which he could not understand by his own thoughts. He prepared himself for the journey home, thinking that there were many other large and clean rivers in his country and that he would be cleansed if he washed himself in any of those. At that moment, Naaman's servants urged their master to obey Elisha's instructions and dip himself in the Jordan River.

For Naaman had a good conscience, the general did not act in his thoughts but instead decided to obey Elisha's instructions, and headed for the Jordan. Among people of a social status equivalent to that of Naaman, how many of them would repent and obey at the urging of their servants or others in a lower position than they are?

As we find in Isaiah 55:8-9, *"For my thoughts are not your thoughts, neither are your ways my ways. As the heavens are higher than the earth, so are my ways higher than your ways and my thoughts than your thoughts,"* when we hold fast to man's thoughts and theory, we cannot obey the Word of God. Let us remember the end of King Saul who had disobeyed God. When we incorporate man's thoughts and do not obey the will of God, this is an act of disobedience, and if we fail to acknowledge our disobedience, we must remember that God will abandon and reject us the way King Saul was abandoned by Him.

We read in 1 Samuel 15:22-23, *"To obey is better than sacrifice, and to heed is better than the fat of rams. For rebellion is like the sin of divination, and arrogance like the evil of idolatry."* Naaman thought twice and decided to shatter his own thoughts and follow the instructions of Elisha, a man of God.

By the same token, we must remember that only when we throw away our disobedient hearts and transform them into hearts of obedience according to the will of God, can we achieve the desires of our hearts.

3. Naaman Obeyed the Word of the Prophet

Following Elisha's instructions, Naaman went down to the Jordan River and washed himself. There were many other rivers that were wider and cleaner than the Jordan, but Elisha's instruction to go to the Jordan carried a spiritual significance. The Jordan River symbolizes salvation, while water symbolizes the Word of God that cleanses people's sin and enables them to reach salvation. (John 4:14). That is why Elisha wanted Naaman to wash himself in the Jordan River that leads him to salvation. No matter how larger and cleaner other rivers may be, they do not lead people to salvation, and have nothing to do with God, and thus in those waters God's work cannot be revealed.

As Jesus tells us in John 3:5, *"[No] one can enter the kingdom of God unless he is born of water and the*

Spirit," by washing himself in the Jordan River, a path has been opened for Naaman to receive forgiveness of his sins and salvation, and meet the living God.

Why, then, was Naaman told to wash himself seven times? The number "7" is a complete number that symbolizes perfection. By instructing Naaman to wash himself seven times, Elisha was telling the general to receive forgiveness for his sins and wholly dwell in the Word of God. Only then will God for whom everything is possible manifest the work of healing and cure any incurable disease.

Therefore, we learn that Naaman received healing for his leprosy, against which either medicine or the might of man was futile, because he obeyed the word of the prophet. On this Scriptures plainly tells us, *"For the word of God is living and active. Sharper than any double-edged sword, it penetrates even to dividing soul and spirit, joints and marrow; it judges the thoughts and attitudes of the heart. Nothing in all creation is hidden from God's sight. Everything is uncovered and laid bare before the eyes of him to whom we must give account"* (Hebrews 4:12-13).

Naaman went before God to whom nothing is impossible, shattered his thoughts, repented, and obeyed His will. As Naaman dipped himself seven times in the Jordan River, God saw his faith, cured him of his leprosy, and Naaman's flesh was restored and became clean like that of a young boy.

By showing us a plain piece of evidence which attests that the healing of leprosy was possible only by His power, God tells us that any incurable diseases can be healed when we please Him with our faith that is accompanied by deed.

Naaman Gives Glory to God

After Naaman was healed of his leprosy, he came back to Elisha, confessed, "Now I know that there is no God in all the world except in Israel...your servant will never again make burnt offerings and sacrifices to any other god but the LORD," and gave glory to God.

In Luke 17:11-19 is a scene in which ten people meet Jesus and are healed of leprosy. Yet, only one of them came back to Jesus, praising God in a loud voice, and threw himself at Jesus' feet and thanked Him. Jesus then asked the man, "Were not all ten cleansed? Where are the other nine? Was no one found to return and give praise to God except this foreigner?" He then told the man, "Rise and go; your faith has made you well." If we receive healing by the power of God, we must not only give glory to God, accept Jesus Christ, and reach salvation, but also live by the Word of God.

Naaman had the kind of faith and deed by which he could be cured of leprosy, an incurable disease of his time.

He had a good conscience to believe in the words of a young servant girl who had been taken captive. He had the kind of faith by which he prepared a precious gift to visit a prophet. He showed the deed of obedience even though the instruction of Prophet Elisha did not agree with his thoughts.

Naaman, a Gentile, had once suffered from an incurable disease but through his disease he met the living God and experienced the work of healing. Anyone who comes before the almighty God and shows his faith and deed will receive answers to all his problems no matter how difficult they may be.

May you possess precious faith, show that faith with deed, receive answers to all your problems in life, and become a blessed saint giving glory to God, in the name of our Lord I pray!

Other powerful books by the same author

Heaven I (As Clear and Beautiful as Crystal)
Heaven II (Filled with God's Glory)

A detailed sketch of the gorgeous living environment the heavenly citizens enjoy in the five levels of heavenly kingdoms

---

The Message of the Cross

An earnest message to all mankind from God, who wishes not even one soul to fall into the depths of hell! You will discover the never-before-revealed account of the cruel reality of Hades and hell

---

Hell

A powerful awakening message for all the people who are spiritually asleep; In this book you will find the reason Jesus is the only Savior and the true love of God

---

Tasting Eternal Life Before Death

The testimonial memoirs of Reverend Dr. Jaerock Lee, who was born again and saved from the valley of death and has been leading an exemplary Christian life

---

The Measure of Faith

What kind of a heavenly place is prepared for you and what kind of crown and rewards will you receive in heaven?
This book provides with wisdom and guidance for you to measure your faith and cultivate the best and most mature faith.